INTERGALACTIC!

150 cosmic jokes about space!

Amanda Li

Illustrated by **Mar**

MACMILLAN CHIL

How do spacemen pass the time on long voyages?
They play astronauts and crosses.

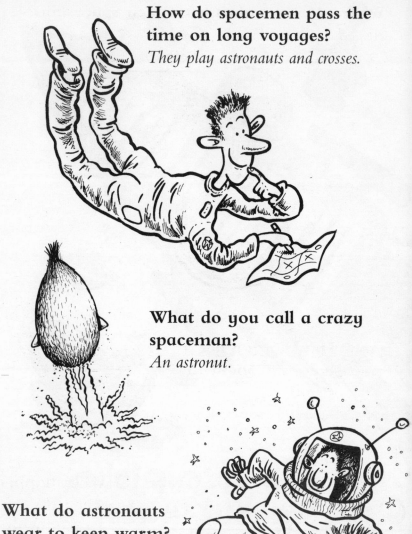

What do you call a crazy spaceman?
An astronut.

What do astronauts wear to keep warm?
Apollo-necked sweaters.

Where do astronauts leave their spaceships?
At parking meteors.

How do you get a baby astronaut to sleep?
Rocket!

What happened when the astronaut found a clock on the moon?
He thought it was a lunar-tick.

What game do astronauts play?
Moon-opoly.

Why do aliens never get hungry in space?
Because they always know where to find a Milky Way, a Mars and a Galaxy.

How does an alien count to nineteen?
On his fingers.

Have you heard the one about the alien bodysnatchers?
I won't repeat it – I might get carried away.

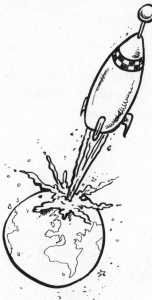

Did you hear the one about the spaceship?
It was out of this world!

Can an alien jump higher than a lamp post?
Yes – lamp posts can't jump.

**Why are aliens
messy tea-drinkers?**
*With flying saucers,
it's hard not to
spill it.*

**Why don't aliens
eat clowns?**
Because they taste funny.

**What did the
alien say to the
plant?**
*Take me to your
weeder!*

**What did the alien say
to the petrol pump?**
*It's rude to stick your finger
in your ear when I'm talking
to you!*

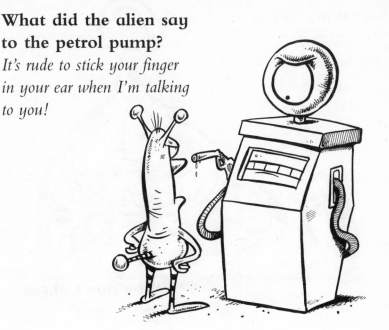

**Alien kids: 'Mum, Mum,
where's our dinner?'**
*Alien mum: 'Be quiet, you lot –
I've only got three pairs of
hands.'*

What are aliens' favourite sweets?
Mars-mallows.

Why did the alien leave the party?
Because there was no atmosphere.

What kind of cheese do robots put on their pizza?
Mars-arella.

What do aliens spread on their toast?
Mars-malade.

Where do Martians buy drinks?
At a Mars Bar.

Why can't aliens learn French?
Because they know no merci!

The famous detective Sherlock Holmes and his friend Dr Watson went on a camping trip.

They set up their tent and fell asleep. During the night, Holmes woke his faithful friend.

'Watson, look up at the sky and tell me what you see.'

Watson replied, 'I see millions of stars.'

'What does that tell you?'

Watson thought for a minute.

'Astronomically speaking, it tells me that there are millions of galaxies and potentially billions of planets. Astrologically, it tells me that Saturn is in Leo. Time-wise, it appears to be approximately a quarter past three. Meteorologically, it seems we will have a beautiful day tomorrow. What does it tell you?'

Holmes was silent for a moment, then he spoke.

'Watson, you idiot, someone has stolen our tent.'

I was up all night
wondering where the
sun had gone . . .
then it dawned on
me!

**What kind
of star is
dangerous?**
*A shooting
star.*

**Why doesn't the
dog-star laugh
at jokes?**
He's too Sirius.

What's a black hole?
What you find in black socks.

When is the
moon heaviest?
When it's full.

What did
Neptune say to
Saturn?
*Give me a ring
sometime!*

15

What did one shooting star say to the other?
Pleased to meteor!

How does a barber cut the moon's hair?
E-clipse it!

Why is there no doorbell on the space station?
They want to win a Nobel Prize!

Why is Saturn called Saturn?
It has a nice ring to it!

What's big, bright and very stupid?
A fool moon.

How does the solar system keep its pants up?
With an asteroid belt!

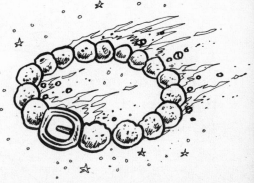

What happens when Saturn gets in the bath?
He leaves a ring around the tub.

What's the opposite of a meteorite?
A meteor-wrong.

What kind of poetry can you find in outer space?
Uni-verse.

What kind of music can you find in outer space?
Nep-tunes.

How do you know that Saturn has been married more than once?
Because he has lots of rings.

Jupiter came down to Earth one day and decided to help two criminals to rob a bank. Anyway, to cut a long story short, they got caught and the three of them found themselves in court. The judge sentenced the two earthlings to fifteen years each in prison, and Jupiter was a bit shocked when he was sentenced to ten years. 'But, Your Honour,' said Jupiter, 'I didn't even take part in the robbery!' 'That may be,' said the judge. 'But you helped them . . . planet!'

What is an astronaut's favourite meal?

Stew, because its 'meaty-all-right'.

What kind of light goes round the Earth?

A satel-lite.

**When is the moon
not hungry?**
When it is full.

**How many astronomers does
it take to change a light bulb?**
None – they're not afraid of the dark!

**What do you call
a space magician?**
A flying sorcerer.

How did the rocket lose his job?
He got fired.

Did you hear about the astronaut who stepped in some chewing gum?
He was stuck in Orbit.

What's brown and travels through time?
Doctor Pooh.

Knock, knock.
Who's there?
Doctor.
Doctor who?
Yes, it's me, and where's my Tardis?

Where does Doctor Who buy his cheese?
At a Dalek-atessen.

Why shouldn't you eat breakfast with a Dalek?
You might get egg-sterminated.

**What does Doctor Who
have with his pizza?**
Dalek bread.

**Why did the
Titanic sink?**
*Because the Doctor
didn't try his Tardis
to save it!*

**How does a Dalek
keep its skin soft?**
Exfoliate!

What do Daleks drink?
Exterminade!

**What do you get if
you cross an alien
and a hot drink?**
Gravi-tea.

What do you call an alien ship that drips water?

A crying saucer!

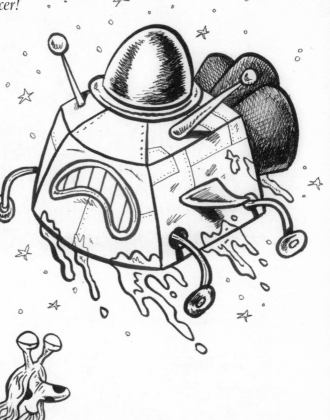

What do you get if you cross a student and an alien?

Something from another universe-ity!

What do you call a sick extraterrestrial?

An ailin' alien.

Why are aliens so scary?

Because they're extra-terror-estrials.

What's an alien's favourite day of the week?
Moonday.

What do aliens eat for breakfast?
ET bix.

What do aliens cook their sausages in?
An Unidentified Frying Object.

**What live on
other planets and
are covered in
tomato sauce?**
Beans from outer space.

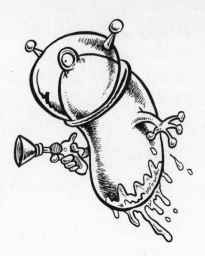

**Why are annoying
aliens like bogeys?**
*They're small, green and
get right up your nose.*

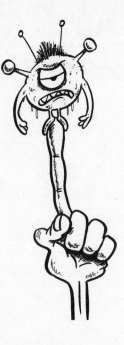

**What should you
do if you meet a
blue alien?**
Try to cheer it up.

**What should you
do if you meet a
green alien?**
Wait until it's ripe.

**What should you
do if you meet a
one-legged alien?**
Tell him to hop it.

**What do you call
a ten-metre-tall
alien with five eyes
and huge teeth?**
Sir.

What does it say on the lid of an astronaut's sandwich box?
Lift off before eating.

An alien walked into a cafe and asked for a cup of tea.
'That'll be a pound, please,' said the waitress when she brought it to him. 'You know, I was just thinking, we don't get many aliens in here . . .'
'I'm not surprised,' said the alien, 'at a pound a cup.'

Why do astronauts wear bullet-proof vests?

To protect themselves against shooting stars.

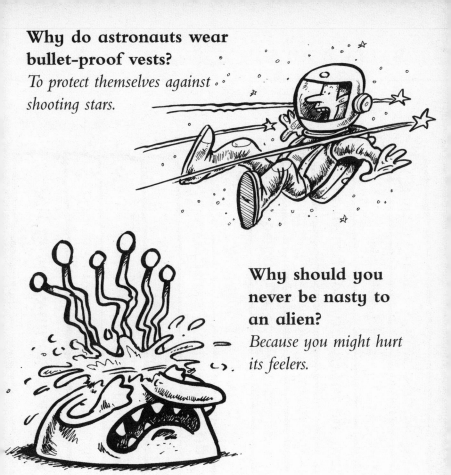

Why should you never be nasty to an alien?

Because you might hurt its feelers.

What did the eyeless alien say to his wife?

I've no idea. (I've no eye, dear.)

BATTY BOOKS

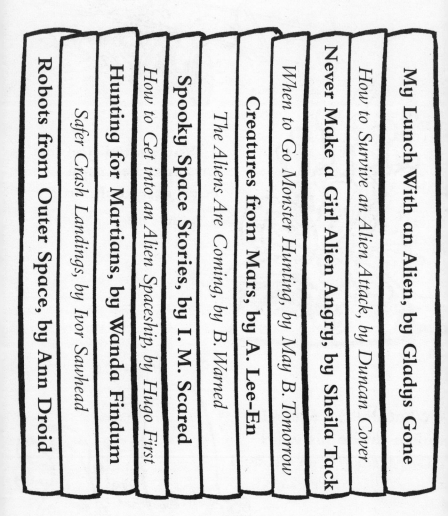

Robots from Outer Space, by Ann Droid

Safer Crash Landings, by Ivor Sawhead

Hunting for Martians, by Wanda Findum

How to Get into an Alien Spaceship, by Hugo First

Spooky Space Stories, by I. M. Scared

The Aliens Are Coming, by B. Warned

Creatures from Mars, by A. Lee-En

When to Go Monster Hunting, by May B. Tomorrow

Never Make a Girl Alien Angry, by Sheila Tack

How to Survive an Alien Attack, by Duncan Cover

My Lunch With an Alien, by Gladys Gone

What happens to astronauts who misbehave?
They're grounded.

What is an astronaut's favourite key on a computer keyboard?
The space bar.

Why are astronauts successful people?
Because they always go up in the world.

How did the aliens hurt the farmer?
They trod on his corn.

How do you greet a three-headed alien?
Hello, hello, hello.

How do Martians throw a party?
They planet.

A woman at a petrol station saw a spaceship landing nearby. An alien stepped out of the spaceship and started to fill it up with petrol. The woman noticed the letters UFO printed on the side of the spaceship. She turned to the alien and asked, 'Does UFO stand for Unidentified Flying Object?' The alien answered, 'No, it stands for Unleaded Fuel Only!'

What's the worst day of the week to meet a hungry space monster?
Chewsday.

How do you keep a huge space monster from charging?
Take away its credit cards.

What should you do if you find a huge space monster in your bed?
Sleep on the sofa.

Did you hear the one about the space monster who ate a whole family?
That's a little hard to swallow.

What did the alien's mum say to him when he got home late?

Where on Earth have you been?

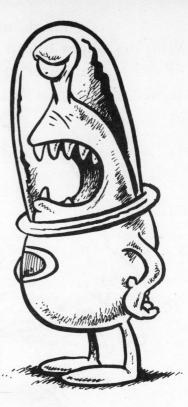

What's the difference between a spaceship and a biscuit?

You can't dunk a spaceship in your tea.

Why are aliens green?

Because they forget to take their travel-sickness tablets.

Knock, knock.
Who's there?
Jupiter.
Jupiter who?
Jupiter hurry – it's freezing out here.

Nurse: Doctor, there's an invisible alien here to see you.
Doctor: Tell him I can't see him.

What's the best way to speak to a space monster?
From a very long way away!

Did you hear about the alien who had eight arms?
He said they came in handy.

Which *Star Wars* character is evil, wears a helmet and goes 'Quack'?
Duck Vader.

Which *Star Wars* character works at a restaurant?
Darth Waiter.

Two Martians were travelling through the solar system when they suddenly felt hungry. They landed on Earth, but had no Earth money, so they decided to steal some sweets from the local shop.

'Stop! You didn't pay for those!' shouted the shopkeeper.

The aliens dropped the sweets and quickly beamed back up to their spaceship. But their alien pals were furious when they discovered they hadn't brought any food back with them.

'What?!' they shouted. 'You couldn't even take a few sweets from a shop without getting caught? What happened?'

'I don't know how the shopkeeper saw us . . .' said one of the unsuccessful shoplifters. 'She must have had eyes in the front of her head!'

How long does Luke Skywalker need to sleep?
One Jedi night.

Which side of an Ewok has the most fur?
The outside.

How did Darth Vader know what Luke Skywalker had for Christmas?
He had felt his presents.

What do Jawas have that no other creature in the Galaxy has?
Baby Jawas.

Who is old, wise and green all over?
Bogey-Wan Kenobi.

Why do doctors make the best Jedi?
Because a Jedi must have patience.

What did Obi-Wan say to Luke at dinnertime?
May the forks be with you.

What holds up the moon?
Moonbeams.

What is the centre of gravity?
V!

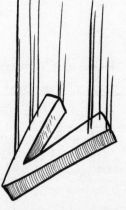

What do planets read?

Comet books.

What did the alien say to the puzzle?

I come in peace; you come in pieces!

What would you do if you saw a spaceman?
Park in it, man!

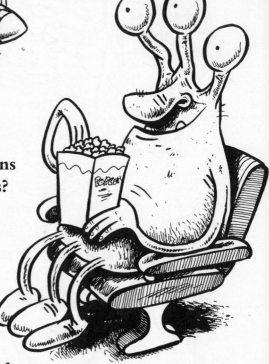

Where do Martians go to watch films?
Cine-Mars.

What comes in a jar and some aliens love it, but other aliens hate it?
Mars-mite.

Why do astronauts make great party guests?
They always have a blast.

Who are the slowest creatures in space?
Snail-iens.

Why do aliens make excellent gardeners?
Cos they've all got green fingers.

Knock, knock.
Who's there?
Jupiter.
Jupiter who?
Jupiter spaceship on my lawn?

How do you know if there's an alien in your house?

There's a spaceship parked in your garden.

How do you know when an alien is jealous?

It turns even greener!

Where do aliens live?

In greenhouses.

What do aliens switch on every Saturday?

Sat-ellites.

Which is the largest sea?
The Galax-sea.

Which is heavier, a full moon or a half moon?
A half moon, because a full moon is lighter!

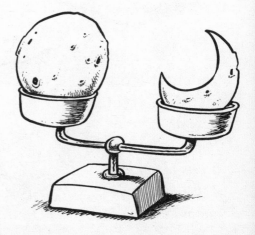

Teacher: How can you prove that the Earth is round?
Pupil: I never said it was, sir!

Pupil: I want to be an astronaut when I grow up.
Teacher: What high hopes you have!

Teacher: How fast does light travel?
Pupil: I dunno, but it gets to my house really early every morning.

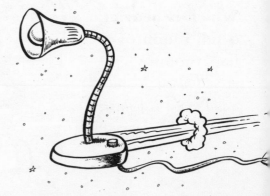

Did you hear about the robot who lived on bits of metal?
It was his staple diet.

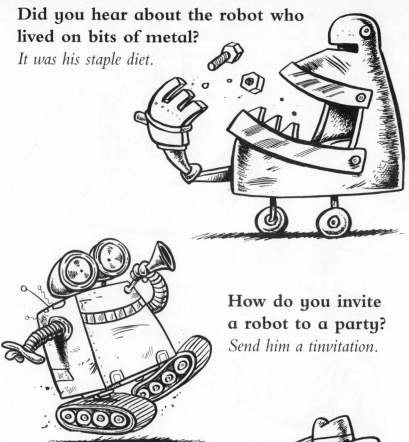

How do you invite a robot to a party?
Send him a tinvitation.

What's a robot's favourite film?
Raiders of the Lost Spark.

What did the mummy robot say to her kids?

Look before you bleep.

How does a robot shave?

With a laser blade.

Do robots have sisters?

No, just transistors.

How does a robot know he's attractive?
When bits of metal stick to him.

Why do robots have so many friends?
They have magnetic personalities.

How do you communicate with aliens in deep space?
You shout really loud!

What's green and very noisy?
An alien with a drum kit.

**What's brown
and travels
through space?**
A Pooh-F-O.

**What do
hungry aliens
travel in?**
A Chew-F-O.

What do aliens put on their cakes?
Mars-ipan.

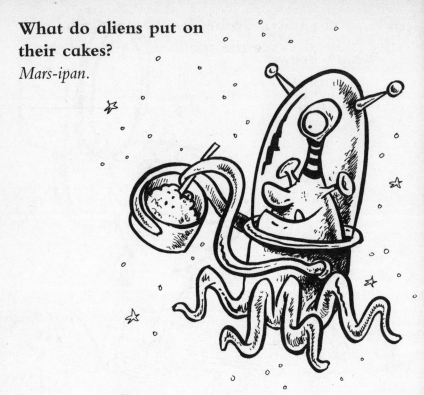

Where do aliens go to study?
Mooniversity.

What must aliens do before they can pilot a spaceship at twice the speed of light across the universe?

Reverse it out of the garage!

Other titles in the *Sidesplitters* series for you to enjoy: